33
Moments Every Parent
Forgets to Enjoy

A Heartfelt reminder to Less Yelling, More Connection, and the Moments You'll Miss One Day

Carrie Khang

Before You Begin...
Grab Your Free Gift

Do mornings in your house sometimes start with rushing, repeating, and eventually... yelling?

You're not alone. Many loving parents lose their patience during the morning rush.

Download my free guide **"Stop the Morning Yelling"** and learn **6 simple steps to create calmer mornings for your whole family.**

https://carriekhang.com

Other Books by Carrie Khang:

Introduction

(Before You Start Counting)

This is not another parenting manual.

There are already too many people who tell you how to parent, and why you are not doing it quite right.

Instead, I would like you to think of this book as a pause button. So, press pause. Remind yourself that in between the spilt milk, the lost socks, the never-ending requests for one more bedtime story, there is a tiny little miracle taking shape right under your exhausted nose.

The reality is that, when you are a busy parent, most of them do not look like miracles at the time.

Instead, they look like noise, mess, delays, and sleepless nights. Exactly the kind of chaos that you would trade your right hand to escape from for even five minutes.

And then, one day, when all that is left is silence, you quietly wish that you could trade that same right hand to hear "Mom!" again.

This book will talk more about the 33 small things you'll want to
remember later.

These are the moments that do not show up in highlight reels or
baby books. These are the ones that don't feel very important until
you can't experience them anymore.

Instead of telling you to slow down, meditate or color-coordinate
your life, this book asks you to notice.
Simply notice. Smile, even if it is for half a second.

Because it is in these tiny, imperfect, ordinary moments that you
are building a childhood that they will always remember. And one
day - the memories you'll ache for.

No deep breathing required. Just turn the page

What's Waiting For You

1–10 | Everyday Little Moments

1. The way your child says your name when they're half asleep.

2. Sticky morning hugs before school.

3. The sound of little feet running through the house.

4. Waiting in the car while they tell you "just one more thing."

5. The smell of their shampoo after bath time.

6. Watching them concentrate with their tongue sticking out.

7. Their wild bedhead in the morning.

8. Crayons left on the table after a creative storm.

9. Hearing them laugh from another room.

10. Seeing Your Own Face on Theirs.

11–20 | Connection & Growing Up

11. When they still reach for your hand in public.

12. The way they sneak into your bed on stormy nights.

13. The long bedtime stories that never seem to end.

14. The messy art projects that ruined the table — and your heart a little.

15. Their "I'm sorry" hugs that melt everything.

16. The silly songs you made up together.

17. The way they light up when you clap for them.

18. How they still want you to kiss the "boo-boos."

19. Their first proud attempt at making you breakfast.

20. The chaos of family dinner — and how full the table feels.

21–27 | Growing Independence & Everyday Love

21. The way they call for you when they're scared.

22. Watching them sleep, realizing how much they've grown.

23. All the "Why?" questions that used to drive you crazy.

24. When they tell you a secret like it's the biggest thing in the world.

25. The way they still believe you can fix anything.

26. The way they yell "I did it!" when they finally succeed.

27. Their funny mispronunciations you'll miss one day.

28–33 | Reflection, Letting Go & Remembering

28. The messy mornings that always make you late.

29. Their first time riding a bike without training wheels.

30. The way they defend you, even when they're mad at you.

31. Family movie nights that turn into popcorn fights.

32. That they still believe in magic — and maybe you should, too.

33. Realizing that these ordinary days were the big moments all along.

THESE ARE THE MOMENTS
THAT MAKE UP A CHILDHOOD.
LET'S PAUSE LONG ENOUGH
TO NOTICE THEM.

01
The Way Your Child Says Your Name
When They're Half Asleep

This is the one that you often hear late at night. The soft, sleepy voice that calls your name.

This is not the same voice that argued with you before bedtime, trying to negotiate its way around extra screen time.

This voice is different, and if you really listen, you will hear that it is quiet, tender, and filled with an unmistakable sense of love and trust.

When you hear this soft, sleepy voice, you will be tired. You may even be annoyed that you had finally sat down to rest your weary legs, only to be needed again.

But then you see them, and any feelings of annoyance immediately dissipate. Cheeks warm, hair messy, head softly lying against the pillow, eyes barely open. Immediately you realize – they were not calling you because they wanted anything. They just needed to know that you were near.

It is at that very moment that the noise and chaos of the day begin to fade. You skim through the ways in which you had wished you had handled those moments better.

You know, without a doubt, that this small voice sees you as their safety, their comfort, their home.

One day, those soft sleepy voices won't be calling your name anymore. But tonight, they still are. And that's something sacred.

Tiny habits to remember this moment:

- When you hear that sleepy call, take a second to pause before reacting. Then, take a slow breath, and whisper back, *"I'm here."*
- Rest your hand gently on their head for a few seconds after tucking them in. Let the stillness wash over both of you.
- This stillness, and the feeling of your soft touch on their warm head is a moment of quiet repair. And, even if the day was messy, or you yelled more than you should have, there are no words needed. Just presence.

These small moments are the ones that leave something lasting in both of you. They won't last forever, but they will forever be a reminder that that says, *even when I was tired, I showed up.*

02
Sticky Morning Hugs
Before School

As the sun rises, you know that it is going to be another morning of chaos. The case of the missing shoe, the burnt toast, the lost homework.

And then, just as you are counting the minutes, and worrying about how late you are going to be, a small syrup-covered pair of arms wraps around you.

As your eyes widen, and you feel the stickiness on your shirt, your first instinct may be to pull away and say, *not now, I don't have time for this.*

But...before you do. Stop for just a second. That sticky hug? It is the most honest part of your morning. It is them saying...*before you rush away into your world, let me hold you for a moment in mine.*

One day, these honest hugs will be short lived, or non-existent, and they'll run out the door without looking back. And then you will be alone. The mornings will be quiet. You'll have all the time you have ever wished for, but you'll miss this mess.

Let them. Let them hug you even if it stains your outfit. Let them smear a little jelly on your sleeve. Let them remind you that connection will always matter more than being on time.

⭐ Tiny habits to remember this moment:

- When they run up to wrap their arms around you before they go to school...Stop. Don't multitask. Hug them like you mean it. Hug them like they are the only thing in your world at that moment.
- Say one kind thing before they leave: "I love how ready you are for today," or "You make my mornings better and brighter."
- On the days when you have had a really rough start, allow that hug to be the reset button. It's never too late to begin the day again, with warmth and tenderness.

The mornings are not always going to run smoothly. But that is not the thing that they are going to remember. They are going to remember your arms wrapped around their little bodies, your warm smile, and how you always made the time for a hug, even on the mornings that were filled with chaos.

03
The Sound of Little Feet Running
Through the House

○○○

That quick and uneven pitter patter that you hear heading your way before you even see them. The sound echoes every day when they are small. It can be chaotic, and sometimes even loud, but that is also the sound of life.

There will come a day when shoes stay neatly by the door, and the house is quiet. There will be no more little footsteps and giggles racing down the hallway to find you. And those thumps that once made you sigh...you will miss them.

While you may be used to saying, *"Stop running inside!"*, why not let them run once more. Down the hallway, and into your arms. You can still tell them to stop running down the hall tomorrow.

Those little feet pattering around the house are not just noise. It is proof that your home is alive and filled with joy and laughter. Proof that they are growing and thriving.

Tiny habits to remember this moment:

- Your immediate reaction would be to say, "Don't run," but stop yourself, and say this "I love how excited you are!".

After that you can even run with them up and down the hallway for a few seconds.

- Record their laughter every now and then. As they grow up and move on, that sound will be a time capsule you'll treasure later.
- When the chaos is over and the house is quiet, pause and acknowledge how very privileged you have been to live through that beautiful noise.

The silence. One day it will come. But right now, let those little feet run and let your heart keep up.

Those days. The days that you have already parked, and the car engine is off. Your mind will be three steps ahead. You will be thinking about what you need to get for dinner, or maybe that pressing email that you haven't yet answered.

You are rushing them out of the car, and then you hear it: "Mom, wait... just one more thing."

You freeze, then turn your head sightly, ready to say, *"Can we talk about it later?"* But there is just something in their voice that stops you from uttering those words. It's never really "just one more thing."
It's *something important disguised as small talk.*
A story they couldn't finish at the dinner table.
A question that they were too shy to ask you earlier.
A tiny piece of their heart they're handing you while the world outside the car stays still.

And as the car automatically turns into a safe place, a kind of neutral ground, no eye contact needed, no distractions. It is in these moments that you don't have to fix or teach. You just need to listen. All that is needed is your quiet presence and their voice.

⭐ Tiny habits to remember this moment:

- Remember that the best parts always come right after you have said goodbye. So, when they say, "One more thing," stay in your seat, and let the silence stretch.
- Consider keeping a small note on your dashboard that says, *"Listen before you rush."* You will never regret these moments.
- Car rides are not interruptions. They are mini conversations. Most of what really matters is said in those ordinary in-between moments.

There is going to be a day that they are driving themselves around. And, you'll turn your head to that empty seat, wishing that there was just one more story to make you late.

05

The Smell of Their Shampoo

After Bath Time

Bath time isn't always the most peaceful routine.
Both you and the floor are soaked, and they are splashing like they are in a theme park.

You keep saying, "Don't get water on the floor!" and they do it anyway, all while you are thinking about the dishes or the laundry still waiting.

But then, as quickly as it starts, the chaos comes to an end. You gently wrap them in a towel. They are warm, slippery, and smell like soap and sweetness. Their hair is damp against your neck as you carry them out. You breathe in, and for a moment, you feel absolute peace.

And do you know what you will remember?

The scent of their shampoo, their clean skin, the way they rest against you like they still fit perfectly in your arms. And even though the evening has been long and messy, you are now reaping its quiet reward.

Later, when it's time to get clean and there are only showers behind closed doors, you'll miss this version. You will miss the puddles, the giggles, the soft "Mommy, dry me."

⭐ Tiny habits to remember this moment:

- Stop yourself from rushing to the next thing that you need to do and instead take a minute. One slow minute. Sit with them. Brush their hair and lotion their arms, and breathe them in.
- Let them help you clean up the splashes, sing a song as you go, and turn the entire experience into teamwork.
- Whisper sweet nothings into their ears as you wrap their little bodies in the towel. Tell them: "You smell like home," or "You make this mess worth it."

It's not about the perfect bath routine. It is about how they feel when it is over: safe, warm, and loved.

06
Watching Them Concentrate with
Their Tongue Sticking Out

Then there are the days when they are sitting at the table, clutching a pencil, and drawing something that only makes sense to them. You see their tongue poking out. Their eyes are narrowed in focus, as the rest of the world just fades away.

Your first instinct is to step in. To guide them, correct them, help them.

But then, something stops you. You realize that this little human is trying to figure things out on their own.

You think back to the times when you are doing something difficult as well. It could be trying not to burn dinner, fixing something that is broken, or even holding back frustration.

It's the same thing. You are both just learning patience, but in different ways.

And then, you smile. You continue to stand nearby but say nothing. It is at that moment that you understand that love means letting them try, even when it is slow or wrong at first.

Later, when they run up to you and proudly show you their drawing or paper plane, you can clearly see the effort that has been put into it.

That little tongue, the deep focus, and the courage that they had to keep going makes you understand that is how you want them to see you as well.

Still learning. Still trying. Still growing together.

⭐ Tiny habits to remember this moment:

- Instead of following your instincts and jumping in to fix what they are doing, take a pause. Breathe, and just watch them.
- Tell them that you love how hard they are working. But you don't need to say, "That's perfect." Everything that you are doing right now teaches them that effort matters.
- Remember that you both need patience. Give it to them...and to yourself.

It's not just about what they're making.
It's about who they're becoming and how watching them makes both of you gentler.

Their Wild Bedhead
in the Morning

Mornings are buzzing with chaos, and often not very pretty. You will find yourself half-awake, juggling to get breakfast and backpacks ready while constantly glancing at the clock.

Then they walk it. Their hair is sticking up in every direction, and their eyes are barely open, as if they are still wrapped up in their dreams.

You want to tell them to go and brush their hair right away. But if you just stop and take a breather, you will notice that their wild hair and sleepy faces are the most real version of them. No performance, no rush, no pretending. Just your little one, as they are.

They lean onto the counter and mumble something about breakfast, while still wearing their mismatched socks, and for a moment, you will take it all in. You will realize how small they still are — even when they act big.

The time will come when they care about their hair. There will come days when they close the bathroom door and fix every strand, rolling their eyes when you reach out to smooth it for them.

But right now, at this very moment, you can smooth their hair, and they will let you. Right now, they still belong to the soft, slow mornings where love looks like cereal, messy hair, and sleepy hugs.

Tiny habits to remember this moment:

- Give them a big morning hug before trying to fix their hair. Start the day with connection, not direction.
- On those mornings, when your head is already thumping and everything feels like chaos, stop, pause, and then really look at them. This is what "home" looks like.
- Take a snapshot with your mind. You don't need a picture for your phone, but rather for your heart. Before you know it, you will look back on their messy hair and wish that you could mess it up again.

It is this messy hair, sleepy hugs, and crumbs on the counter that are at the very heart of childhood. And perhaps the softest part of parenthood, too.

08

Crayons Left on the
Table After
a Creative Storm

You walk into the living room, and the table is a mess again. Paper scraps are lying everywhere, open markers without their caps, pencil shavings lying under the chairs, and you let out a big sigh. You have only just cleaned the living room an hour ago, and now it looks like a hurricane has hit.

Before you start picking up the mess, just stop and look at it for a second. Instead of a mess, you will see a trail of imagination. Half-drawn rainbows, stick figures, family portraits. This is not simply a mess. This is proof that their minds are busy and that they feel free enough to put their thoughts on paper.

All along, your purpose has been to teach them how to color inside the lines. But maybe they are teaching you something else. To stop trying to make things neat all the time. To allow joy to take up space.

The days of tidy tables will arrive before you know it. But for now, you have a little human, who still believes in purple skies and blue cats.

In fact, you have evidence of wonder scattered across your living room.

Tiny habits to remember this moment:

- Before you start packing away the crayons, take a moment to look at what they have made – look beyond the mess and picture the vision that they had in their minds.
- Ask them to tell you more about what they have drawn. The story behind the drawing often means more than what has been drawn.
- Put a shoe box in your cupboard and keep one doodle a week. One day you'll open the box and realize that it was never clutter — it was memories.

Remember that right now, in this moment, the crayons, the colors, the mess are all proof of a childhood still happening right here, in your ordinary, beautiful home.

09
Hearing Them Laugh
from Another Room

It is another busy day, and it feels like you are washing dishes, returning emails, and folding laundry all at once.

Then, suddenly, you hear it.
That laugh. The kind that bursts out without warning.

You stop what you are doing. You can't see them, but you are picturing the scene. A fallen toy, an inside joke with a sibling, and then a giggle that turns into a full belly laugh.

The laugh that you hear coming right from their bellies is the rare sound that makes everything seem worth it. It softens you, and whatever stress you had weighing down on you fades, even if only for a moment.

Because no matter how tired you are, it is that laughter that reminds you that they are ok. They are still able to find joy and see the light in places you might have stopped noticing.

In a few years, the laughter that you hear from another room will belong to older, deeper, and quieter voices. Or maybe these voices do not even live in the same house anymore.

Revel in the fact that today, that sound is your reminder that your child still feels safe enough to laugh freely under your roof.

⭐ Tiny habits to remember this moment:

- When you hear them laugh, stop whatever you're doing, and allow the sound to sink in. It could be the medicine that you didn't know you needed.
- You don't need to rush to find out what is so funny. Let it stay theirs. It is their joy blooming without you even having to be there – and that means something special.
- Even on your worst days, when things feel heavy, remember this moment, and know that if they are still laughing, then you are doing better than you may think.

That sound from the other room is more than just background noise. It's proof that you have built a home where joy feels easy.

10
Seeing Your Own Face
in Theirs

You are running late, and you roll your eyes at a slow driver.
Later that week, your child rolls their eyes at you in the exact same way.

You sigh loudly when you knock over your coffee.
Later that afternoon, you hear a tiny version of that sigh when the Lego tower falls over.

You say, "Hurry up," a little sharper than you meant.
At bedtime, you hear the same sharp edge when they snap at a sibling: "Hurry up!"

This catches you off guard, and while you might want to correct them, you suddenly realize that they learned it from you.

This is not their way of being rude. This is them trying to be like you. Borrowing your face, your tone, the way you handle frustration.

It's sweet when they copy your laugh, but it can sting when they copy your frustration.

This is one of those quiet growing-up moments that you will never forget. The day you saw your own expressions walking around on a smaller face and decided to soften what they were copying.

⭐ Tiny habits to make this moment count:

- Before you answer them a little too harshly, let your shoulders drop and your voice soften. Repeat in your mind, *"Soft face, soft voice", and* let them copy that version of you.
- Nobody is perfect, but then you do snap, you can repair any damage with one simple sentence: "That came out too sharp. Let me try again." One day, they will use the same line with someone they love.
- Make note of the moments where they copy your calm. Say something like, "I saw you breathe before you answered your brother. That was kind." Let them know that's the part of you worth repeating.

You'll never be a perfect example. No parent is. But when you take the time to soften your own reactions, you're shaping the face and voice they'll carry into their own life.

11
When They Still Reach forYour
Hand in Public

You're making your way across the parking lot of the store with your arms full of grocery bags. You are fumbling for your car keys, and at the same time, your phone is buzzing in your pocket.

Behind you, your kid calls out, "Mom, hand!"

You want to say, "Mom's hands are full!", but you stop yourself before you do.
You turn to them softly and say, "Mommy's hands are full, baby. But you can put your hand in my pocket so we can walk together."

Before you have even finished your sentence, they slide their little hand into your coat pocket, and you both walk. Side by side. Quiet and connected. No lecture. No rush. Just the sound of small feet beside yours and that tiny hand, warm against your hip.

And as you make your way towards the car, you realize it's not about holding hands anymore. It's about staying close and finding new ways to belong to each other as they grow. One day they won't reach out at all, but for now, they still do — and that's something to cherish.

Tiny habits to remember this moment:

- There are going to be times when you can't hold their hand. But remember that there are plenty of other ways to connect. Always let them know that you have an open pocket or a sleeve that they can hold.
- Sometimes it is healthy to let them be the one to reach for you. Connection does not always have to start with the parent.
- That small hand will only be small for a while, so every time you feel it reach for you, stop rushing for a few seconds. That's their way of reminding you to slow down and remember that you are their safe place.

One day, you'll walk to the car alone, swinging empty hands, so take the time to feel that warmth in your pocket.

12
The Way They Sneak into Your
Bed on Stormy Nights

It's late, and lightning crashes. You are half asleep, but you can hear the soft footsteps coming down the hall, and then a whisper. "Mommy, can I come in?"

But before you are even able to answer, that little body has climbed under the blanket, its cold toes brushing your leg. They don't feel the need to say more. All they do is wiggle themselves closer to you until their head finds that familiar spot near your shoulder.

And even though you have read all the advice about how you should send them back to bed, set boundaries, encourage independence – outside it is raining, and in all honesty, you don't mind.

You listen as their breathing starts to slow down and they drift back off to sleep with their little hand tucked in yours. You think back to the days when you used to wish that they would sleep through the night, but now you realize how quickly those nights disappear.

One day, the storms will not send them running to you, and they will learn how to face the thunder on their own. But in this moment, they sincerely believe that being next to you makes everything feel safe.

And maybe they're right.

⭐ **Tiny habits to remember this moment:**

- If they come to your bed scared, there is no need to fix it straight away. First, let them settle and breathe in your calm.
- Whisper, "You're safe, I'm right here." Those four words do more than any nightlight ever could.
- When they eventually drift off to sleep, stay with them for a few minutes longer than you planned. Because one day, you'll wish you could go back to that very moment.

Let them crawl into your bed. Cuddle them. Allow them to need you. It's not weaknesses, it's trust. One day, there will be no more thunder paired with tiny footsteps coming down the hall.

13
The Long Bedtime Stories That
never Seem to End

It's late. You have a big meeting at work in the morning, and you are exhausted.

You've already said goodnight twice, kissed them three times, and turned the light on and off for what feels like the hundredth time.

Then comes the voice. "Mom... can you read one more? Just one more?"

You try your best not to sound annoyed and say, "No, it's late. Tomorrow's school."
But then you see their little face. They look disappointed but still hopeful, still holding the book open to the page where you left off.

You stand in the doorway. You could walk away. After all, that would be the logical choice. But something inside makes you sit down next to them again, and you pick up right where you left off. Except, this time your voice is slower.

They lean in, their eyelids already heavy, and halfway through the first page, their breathing deepens, and you realize that they didn't want the story. They just wanted you.

You close the book and stare at them as they sleep. The to-do list in your head fades. And then it hits you. There is only a small window in life when they still want you beside them like this.

⭐ Tiny habits to remember this moment:

- It's okay to say no sometimes. But occasionally, even if you are tired, say yes.
- If you can't read another page, tell them, "One paragraph and then I'll just sit with you for a bit." It's presence they're really asking for.
- Don't rush out the door after they fall asleep. Take a few moments to look at their peaceful faces while they are sleeping. That's the kind of peace you can carry into your night.

There will one day be nights when the never-ending quiet of an empty home will drive you crazy. You'll have years of quiet nights ahead. But now, you are the last voice that they are going to hear before they fall asleep, and you wouldn't want it any other way.

14
The Messy Art Projects That Ruined the Table —
and Your Heart a Little

You walk into the kitchen and stop mid-step. There's paint everywhere. Glitter on the floor.

You take a deep breath, or maybe you don't.
"Seriously? We just cleaned this table!"
They freeze, brush in hand, eyes wide. "I was making you something."

And just as quickly as your irritation starts, it starts to dissipate. You lean in to take a closer look and see paper hearts, or maybe a rainbow with too many colors that somehow still says "I love you."

As you grab a sponge and start to gently wipe down the paint marks, they rush to your side to help you. They are still babbling about what they were trying to make for you.

You realize you're not just cleaning up a mess — you're cleaning up a memory. The table won't always look like this. Someday it'll be spotless with no paint, no crumbs, and no signs of life.

You'll miss this mess that proves someone small was still learning to find joy right here.

⭐ Tiny habits to remember this moment:

- Before getting angry and scolding, softly ask, "Show me what you were working on." Curiosity slows frustration.
- Keep one art "disaster" a month. Tape it somewhere you can smile at later.
- Turn correction into connection, and when you clean together, talk about the project rather than the mess.

You can always scrub the paint later. But you cannot always get back to the moment when they still wanted to show you what their heart looked like in color.

15
Their "I'm Sorry" Hugs
That Melt Everything

It starts with raised voices, slammed doors, and maybe even a few tears. You said something that you didn't mean, and they yelled back, something that they have picked up from you.

At first, both of you are too stubborn to give in.

Then, a little while later, you hear the familiar footsteps. They appear in the doorway with their head down, eyes wet, voices small. "I'm sorry."

But, before you can even answer, their arms wrap tight around your waist.

You want to hold on to the anger for a bit so that you can make your point. You want to remind them that what they did was wrong.

But then you feel it. That little squeeze, the shaky breath against your chest, and all your reasons fade. You bend down, hug back, and whisper, "Me too."

That hug is repair in its purest form. Not words, not lectures. Just love saying, *we can start again.*

And the truth is, you're not just forgiving them. You are forgiving yourself as well. For being human. For forgetting that this relationship is much bigger than any argument ever will be.

⭐ Tiny habits to remember this moment:

- Hug first, talk later. When they come to say sorry, don't rush to teach. Receive it with open arms.
- After a big fight, take turns telling one another one thing you still love about each other. It rewires how they see mistakes.
- Say out loud, "We both lost our cool, but I love you anyway." That's how they learn real repair.

One day, they'll know how to offer this same kind of grace because they saw it in you. Your job is to teach them that love isn't about never breaking — it's about always coming back.

This one is definitely not planned.

You could be brushing your teeth or waiting for the traffic light to turn green when you both burst into a ridiculous song.

The words may not even make sense.
"Brushy-brushy sparkle power!"
"Left shoe, right shoe, don't forget your lunch!"

They start to giggle so hard that they can't breathe, and that makes you laugh too. You secretly know that even though you know you sound ridiculous, it is not about the song.

It's about the rhythm — the rhythm that holds a family together during all the small in-between moments.

Weeks later, they'll hum your made-up tune while packing their backpack or walking upstairs, and you'll freeze for a second — realizing it stuck. That silly moment. The one that you almost forgot became a part of their world.

You may not remember every lyric, but they will. They'll always remember laughing with you for no reason. That the world felt right in that very moment.

⭐ Tiny habits to remember this moment:

- When the normal day-to-day routine gets too much, add a song. Music has the unique ability to turn resistance into play.
- Record one of your silly duets on your phone. One day, it will make you cry — in a good way.
- Don't worry about sounding good. Joy doesn't need a tune.

You don't have to sing like you are in a band. All you need to do is join in.

Because one day, they'll be too old for silly songs, but they will always remember the sound of your laughter in between the lyrics.

17

The Way They Light
Up When
You Clap for Them

"Watch this!"
Those two words have been on repeat at least ten times in the last
half an hour.

It could be a cartwheel that is not really a cartwheel, a joke that
has not quite landed, or even the belly flops into the pool that they
insist is the best dive in the world.

You are sitting by the pool, answering an email, but you still look
up, and you clap!

Their whole face lights up like you just handed them the world.
They jump, laugh, and yell, "Did you see that?!"
And yes, you did. Even if it wasn't perfect. Even if you were tired.
You still clapped — and that meant everything.

The truth is that children don't want applause for performance.
They want proof that you *noticed*. That you saw them trying,
creating, and being brave.

One day, their "watch this!" will stop, and it will sound more like
"Can I show you something?" or "What do you think?"

Don't miss those moments, either. It's still the same child underneath, just a little taller, still craving your eyes and your approval.

Tiny habits to remember this moment:

- Attention is louder than applause. When they say, "watch this," always remember to look up. Even if it is only for a few seconds.
- Praise the effort, not the outcome. Say "You worked hard on that!" instead of "That was perfect!"
- Keep on cheering, even as they get older. Everyone still needs someone who claps for them.

Remember, your applause is how they learn that they matter. They don't need you to be impressed; they just need you to be *present*.

18
How They Still Want You to
Kiss the 'Boo-Boos'

You hear the tears before you even know what happened.
A fall on the driveway. A stubbed toe. Maybe a bump on the shin that doesn't even leave a mark.

And you sigh.
From the kitchen window, you call out, "You're fine! Get up!"
But they don't. They keep crying, and running toward you with their arms outstretched.

By the time you see their teary face, you can see it. Not just the scrape on the knee, but the fear.

You kneel down, still half-annoyed, and say, "Let me see."
They sniffle, point to the spot like it's serious. "It really hurts mommy."
You almost say, "It's nothing," but instead, you lean in and kiss it.

And, just as if it has never happened, the boo boo has been fixed. The tears stop, and the world is okay again.

You shake your head, half-smiling. You know that they didn't need first aid- they just needed you!

Because it is your voice. Your touch. Your calm that tells them everything's fine.

One day, their world will feel so much bigger, and you won't always be able to fix it for them.

But right now, you still are, and these are the moments that need to be treasured.

Tiny habits to remember this moment:

- When you want to say, "You're fine," try to stop yourself, and kneel in front of them instead. It is that kind of connection that heals faster than logic.
- Say, "That must've hurt," before you fix it. Always practice empathy first, and lessons later.
- Hug them for a little longer. They'll remember your arms long after they forget the scrape.

You'll spend years teaching them to be brave.
But today, let them be small. Let your kiss be enough.

19
Their First Proud Attempt at
Making You Breakfast

You walk into the kitchen only to find that the counter is covered in crumbs. There is milk on the floor, and pancake mix everywhere — even on the dog.

Your first thought isn't *aaaw how sweet.*
It's *oh no!*

You stare at the mess in front of you, already contemplating how long the cleanup is going to take. *Who's cleaning this up?*

Then you see them, standing on a chair, spatula in hand, proud and nervous. "Mom! I made you breakfast!"

You want to say something about the mess, but you stop yourself.

Because behind the flour on their face and the sticky counter, you see it. The effort, the love, the purest form of "I thought of you."

You sit down, take a bite of your pancakes, and smile.
It's cold. It's uneven. It's perfect!

You know that you have a big job ahead and that the kitchen is not going to tidy itself.
But one day, this won't happen anymore.

One day, they'll sleep late. They'll rush out the door with headphones on. They won't wake up early just to surprise you with breakfast.

And you'll wish you could walk back into this messy kitchen just one more time.

⭐ Tiny habits to remember this moment:

- When you walk into the kitchen, your initial thought will be to react. But take a breather and look for the heart behind it first.
- Take a picture of them covered in pancake mix— not for Instagram, just for yourself. One day, that picture will mean so much more.
- Let them help you clean but keep your tone light and remember that connection lasts longer than scolding.

You'll have plenty of clean kitchens in the years ahead.
But none that hold this kind of love in the mess.

20
The Chaos of Family Dinner —
and How Full the Table Feels

It's been a long day. You sit at the dinner table. It is loud and busy.

Someone's complaining about the food. Someone else is spilling water. You're trying to get everyone to sit down at the same time, but the dog's barking, someone can't find a fork, and the youngest just announced they "don't like this anymore."

You sigh as you look around the table and think to yourself, *can we just have one peaceful meal?*

But later, as the evening winds down. When the dishes are finally done and the house is quiet, you will walk past that same messy table. You will notice the crumbs, the half-empty glasses, the napkins crumpled into little piles.

And then something hits you.

That chaos that surrounded you a few hours ago. That was the sound of a house that is filled with love and growing kids.

There will come a time that everyone will eat on different schedules. You'll make dinner, and the house will stay spotless, but the silence will feel heavy.

You'll miss the noise.
The interruptions.
Even the complaints.

Because underneath it was all about family. Imperfect, messy, but real.

Tiny habits to remember this moment:

- When you take a seat at the dinner table, expect the noise. This noise is proof of togetherness.
- Ask everyone their day. The good parts and the bad. This turns chaos into connection.
- When dinner feels exhausting, remember that this noise means they're still here, still yours.

One day the dinner table is going to seem quiet and lonely. Concentrate on how it is now. Full and busy.

And that's exactly how it's supposed to be.

You hear it from the other room. The panicked "Moooom!"
Your initial thought is, *they can't possibly need me again.*

Then comes the second call, a little sharper this time.
"MOM! Come here, quick!"
You drop everything that you are doing as your motherly instincts
set in, and you rush to them — heart racing, ready for an
emergency.

And then you see it.
A tiny spider.
Sitting quietly minding its business on the corner of the wall.

They're standing on the bed. Their eyes are wide, and they are
clutching a stuffed animal like it's a shield.
You sigh. "Really? It's just a spider."
They shake their head. Their faces are serious. "It was *looking* at
me!"

You try not to roll your eyes, and instead, grab a tissue, scoop it
up, and put it outside. "There. All gone."
They still won't move until you say, "It's safe now."
Then they finally relax, shoulders dropping, and whisper, "Thanks,
Mom."

But your heart feels full. Because one day, no one will call for you like this anymore.

They'll be taller, braver, and perhaps maybe even laugh at you for fearing certain things.

But at this very moment, you are still the one they trust to chase away the monsters — real or imaginary. One day you will miss that little voice calling your name, believing you can fix anything.

Tiny habits to remember this moment:

- Even if you are annoyed that the big emergency that you rushed to was in fact only a little emergency, remember that you are not just calming them — you're teaching safety.
- Instead of telling them not to be scared rather say, "I know that startled you." It validates instead of shaming their fears.
- Write down one "Mom!" or "Dad!" moment each week so that you can look back on them one day when the silence feels too big.

You'll handle a thousand small fears. Spiders, dark corners, monsters.

But someday, you'll wish you could hear that tiny voice one more time saying, "Mom… come here. I need you"

22
Watching Them Sleep, Realizing
How Much They've Grown

You rush into their rooms, just to grab some laundry or turn off the light.

And, then you see them. Sprawled out across the bed. Blanket half off, one arm hanging over the edge, breathing slow and even.

For a moment, you just stand there and stare at their faces. Because you have just realized that they don't look like your little kid anymore.

Their faces have changed. Less baby. More grown. You stand there a little longer and notice their long legs, and the messy hair that suddenly looks older.

And then you close your eyes and think back to the nights you used to rock them to sleep. The tiny body that once fitted snugly in your arms.

You used to wish for longer stretches of sleep, for this very stage you're in now. But now that it's here, it feels... too fast.

You whisper, "Goodnight," even though they can't hear you. You brush the hair from their forehead, the same way you've done since they were small.

Then you turn off the light and stand in the doorway just a little longer. Holding that quiet ache in your chest that only a parent can understand.

And that's when it hits you. Growing up doesn't happen in big leaps. It happens in inches. It's in the small things you almost miss until you're standing there, watching them sleep, wondering when the change happened.

⭐ Tiny habits to remember this moment:

- Take as many pictures as you can while they are growing up. One day you are going to want to remember every moment.
- Allow yourself to feel. Let yourself linger for a minute before leaving their room. Stillness is part of parenting, too.
- When you feel the ache, don't rush it away. It is your love that is growing with them.

One day you will blink and that bed will be empty. So just for tonight, wait a little longer. Watch a little closer.
Because this, right not, right here, in the quiet — is what "too fast" feels like.

23

All the "Why?" Questions That
Used to Drive You Crazy

"Why is the sky blue?"
"Why do dogs have tails?"
"Why can't I have dessert first?"
"Why do you have lines on your forehead?"

Before this phase, you used to think nothing could test your patience more than bedtime.
The endless whys. The nonstop curiosity. The way every answer always seems to lead to another question.

There will be some days where you try to explain, and other days where you say, "because that's just how it is," while you juggle the dishes silently praying for quiet.

But it will stop.
At first you may not notice it, as the questions get replaced by silence.
Instead, they start Googling things, talking to friends, or rolling their eyes instead of asking you.

That is when you will miss those little voices that once believed you knew *everything*.

One day you will understand that those questions weren't just about learning about the world. They were about learning *you*.

They asked because they trusted you had the answers.
Because you were their safe place to wonder out loud.

⭐ Tiny habits to remember this moment:

- Rather than saying "I don't know," replace it with "Let's find out together." Curiosity shared is connection built.
- Keep a list of their funniest "why" questions. Years later this is going to make you smile.
- When you're tempted to shut it down, remember that they won't always ask you first. Let them.

The day will come when they figure out the answers on their own. But for this moment. Let them keep asking. Because each "why" is really another way of saying, *"I trust you."*

24

The Small, Quiet Moments When
They Lean on You

It happens quietly. There is no big hug or announcement.

You are folding laundry on the couch while watching your favorite soap opera. Without a word, they sit beside you.
Not saying much. Just close enough that their shoulder touches yours.

Sometimes, they rest their head for a second before pretending they didn't. Other times, they lean halfway in, testing if it's still okay to need you like that.

You stay still, pretending not to notice. But inside, something soft stirs. You want these moments to last forever. Because you know how rare they are becoming.

You remember when they used to crawl into your lap like it was second nature. Without a thought. When your arms were their entire world.
Now, they're growing. Taller, busier, and full of their own thoughts and feelings.
And yet... here they are, leaning on you again. Not as a baby this time, but as a person who still finds peace in your presence.

Don't move too fast or try to fill the silence. Just let it be what it is. This is the quiet language of love that doesn't need words anymore.

⭐ Tiny habits to remember this moment:

- When they sit close to you, don't rush to talk. Presence says more than advice.
- Put the laundry down for a minute. They can tell when you're really there.
- When they lean in, lean back gently. Let them feel that they still belong here. Right next to you.

One day, they will start to pull away. But that's all part of growing. But for now, stay still. Let them rest against you.

Because sometimes, the softest connections are the ones that need no words.

25

The Way They Still Believe You

Can Fix Anything

"Dad, it broke."

You see their favorite toy with its arm snapped, or wheels bent. Your initial reaction is to say, "Why don't you play more carefully?"

But you stop yourself and say, "Okay. Don't toss it yet. Let me have a look"

You sit at the table together. Tape. A tiny screw. A rubber band. They watch like you're doing surgery, faith written all over their face.

Sometimes the repair works. Sometimes it doesn't. But it is so much more than that. They are learning something bigger than glue. They are learning that when things break, *we try first*.

And, if it can't be fixed, simply say, "Let's thank it and find another way." And suddenly their world feels safe again.

One day there will be things harder to fix than toys. Friend trouble, a bad grade, a broken heart. You wish that they could still hand it to you and say, "Can we fix it?"

⭐ Tiny habits to remember this moment:

- Wait before you head out to replace the toy. Instead, use this as a moment to try and fix it together.
- Keep a small fix-it box and let them be the helper.
- You are teaching them to be resilient by showing them how to try, and that if it still doesn't work, we will find a new plan.

They believe your hands can make everything better. Show them that your hands can also teach them *how* to make things better, too.

26
The Way They Yell "I Did It!"
When They Finally Succeed

It starts with frustration. The same homework problem, the bike that won't balance, or the same Lego tower that keeps collapsing.

You hear the sighs, the grunts, maybe even the little stomp of defeat. "Forget it!" they say.

Part of you wants to step in, and help them fix it, even if you have dinner to cook, dishes to wash, and time is running out.

But you force yourself to hold back — just enough.
You watch them take a breath and try again.

And that's when it happens. Breakthrough, Success.
"I DID IT!" they shout, face glowing with a pride no one could give them but themselves.

Your heart fills with pride. Not because of what they built, but because of what was built *inside* them.

And it is that sound, their joy, their surprise, their belief, that is worth more than any clean kitchen or quiet evening.

✦ Tiny habits that build confidence:

- Remember that growth hides in the space where you allow them to struggle a little longer than what feels comfortable.
- When they succeed, praise the effort, not the result: "You kept trying. That's what made it work!"
- Keep a small "win jar". Fill this jar with all their little triumphs and read them together on tough days.

One day, they will be mature enough to outgrow the sounds of their frustration. But the voice that says *I can do hard things*? That's the one that will stay.

27
Their Funny
Mispronunciations
You'll Miss One Day

"Can I have more *pasketti*?"
"Where's my *hanitizer*?"
"Look, an *aminal!*"

You laugh every time. Sometimes you try to correct them, "It's spaghetti," you say gently.
They repeat, confident: "That's what I said — *pasketti!*"

And you let it go. Because deep down, you know one day they'll say it right, and you'll miss it. The little voices that mispronounce words. The sound of childhood in its purest form.

One day these little word-mix moments will start to happen less. One day, they'll stop calling the refrigerator the "fridge-a-later," or saying "pountin" instead of "fountain."

In fact, their words will become sharper, clearer, more grown-up. And you'll wish you could freeze the way they used to talk. The tiny accent of innocence that only time can erase.

Because that's the thing about growing up. You don't notice the last time they mispronounce a word until it's gone.

Tiny habits to remember this moment:

- Write down the funny ones. Years from now you'll read them and smile through tears.
- When they say it "wrong," repeat it their way once. Let them hear that you enjoy it too.
- Record their little voice occasionally. Your future self will thank you as the memories start flowing back.

So, for now, keep laughing at *pasketti* — and let their little language fill your house while it still can. Their words will grow up long before their hearts do.

28
The Messy Mornings
That Always
Make You Late

It starts the same way every day...
You say, "Let's go!"
No one moves.

They don't seem to have a care in the world. All the while, you are
balancing your coffee, with one shoe on, clutching the car keys and
wondering how it's possible to be late every single morning.

Lost homework. The wrong color socks. The dog that needs to go
out again. The toast that is burnt. You sigh. Loudly!

You mutter things like, "Why can't we ever just leave on time?"
and "This shouldn't be this hard."

You grab backpacks, fix collars, shove shoes on the wrong feet, and
finally herd everyone to the car. By the time you get in the driver's
seat of the car, you feel like you have run a marathon and it is only
7am.

But then. As you're backing out of the driveway, you look in the
rearview mirror.
They're quiet now. The hair is still messy. Mouths are still full of
cereal bars. Someone hums softly to themselves.

And then you feel it. That flicker of warmth in the middle of your
exhaustion.

Because one day, even though you may be able to wake up later in the morning, there will be silence.

No missing shoes. No cereal spills. No burnt toast.

Now you understand that those chaotic mornings were never the problem. They were proof that life was happening, and love was all around, even in the frustrating times.

Tiny habits to remember this moment:

- Before the rush starts, take a deep breath and remind yourself that, "This is what having kids sounds like." And it is beautiful!
- Laugh at one thing every morning. It changes the tone faster than any lecture ever could.
- Snap a quick photo occasionally. Bedheads, backpacks, toothpaste smiles. One day, those are the things that you will miss most.

These mornings may feel endless now, but they are the stories that you will tell when the house is too quiet.

29
Their First Time Riding a
Bike Without Training Wheels

You can almost feel the mix of excitement and fear.
They grip the handlebars a little too tight. Their little legs tremble but they still insist, "Don't hold on, I can do it."

You crouch beside them, steadying the seat.
"Okay, I'll let go when you're ready."
They nod, not looking back.
And then you do it. You let go.

For a second, they wobble, and your anxiety peaks. You hold your breath, hands half raised, ready to catch.
Then suddenly, they are flying. Wobbly, brave, free.
"Look, Mom! I'm doing it!"

And then you feel it. That proud, terrified joy that fills your chest so full it almost hurts.

They don't see you running behind, heart pounding, half cheering, half wanting to grab the bike again. They don't know how much you want to protect them even though you know that you can't.

And then, when they finally fall, you rush over. Not to scold, but to remind them it's okay to fall. To teach them to try again.

So, you quickly brush off their knees, straighten the helmet, and they pedal once more.

There will come a day when you watch them drive away, board a plane, or walk into a new life. It will feel just like this.
You'll want to run behind them again.

But for now, it's just the bike. And that's enough.

Tiny habits to remember this moment:

- Try your best not to jump in too fast when they wobble. Give them the space that they need to find balance.
- Don't just celebrate their success. Celebrate the courage.
- "You were scared, and you tried anyway."
- Keep a tiny piece of that first helmet or knee pad. This is proof of the day you both learned to let go.

Because every "I can do it" begins with you. Running, cheering, and learning how to let them fly.

30
The Way They Defend You, Even When
They're Mad at You

Five minutes ago, you were the "meanest parent ever" because you said no to extra screen time or refused to buy candy at checkout.

They stomped away, muttering under their breath about how they are never going to talk to you again.

But let someone else say something about you.
It could be a classmate joking about how strict you are or a friend teasing them about their dad having a weird job.

And suddenly, your little rebel transforms into your fiercest defender.

"Hey! Don't talk about my mom like that."
"My dad's has the coolest job, actually."

And, when they tell you about it, it catches you off guard.
You think they don't notice how much you do for them. But they do.

And even when the roll their eyes, or slam their door, you realize that love doesn't always sound like "I love you."

Sometimes, it sounds like a quiet defense in a noisy world.

⭐ Tiny habits to remember this moment:

- Anger is often frustration mixed with love, so try not to take their anger at face value.
- When you hear they defended you, don't brush it off. Smile and say, "Thanks for having my back."
- Remember: even when they're mad, you are still their safe place. That's what counts.

They may outgrow the slamming doors, but they will never outgrow the loyalty that built inside them while you stayed steady.

Because deep down, no matter how loud they protest, you are still their person.

31
Family Movie Nights That Turn
Into Popcorn Fights

You are exhausted. It's Friday night, and all you want is a simple quiet family night.

Snacks ready, blankets out, everyone agrees (for once) on a movie. And for about five minutes, it goes smoothly...

And then it happens. Someone wants a different movie. Someone else sits too close. Someone yells, "You're stealing the blanket!"

And just like that, the "relaxing night" you imagined turns into chaos.

Someone throws a handful of popcorn at another in protest. And, before you know it, everyone's laughing, and the movie has been forgotten.

It's not what you planned. It never is. But when you hear the giggles and smell the aroma of a room that smells like butter you understand fully that this is what family feels like. It is not quiet. It is not perfect. But it is full.

Later, when the credits roll, you'll look at their sleepy faces and realize that one day, these spots on the couch will be empty. And you'll wish for one more messy, loud, popcorn-filled night just like this.

⭐ **Tiny habits to remember this moment:**

- The chaos in itself is a memory. You don't need to aim for the perfect movie night. All you need to aim for is togetherness.
- Let them pick the movie sometimes. Even if you hate the movie, it's their turn to feel heard.
- Presence is what makes movie nights magic, so keep the phones away and the lights dim.

Someday, you'll find popcorn under the couch and smile instead of sighing. Because you will remember that they were here. Laughing, arguing, loving, all under one blanket.

32
That They Still Believe in Magic —
and Maybe You Should, Too

Somewhere along the way, we stopped believing in magic, and life became bills, traffic, emails...

But your child hasn't.

They still think the moon follows your car.
They still whisper wishes to candles on their birthdays.
They still believe the Tooth Fairy writes tiny notes and that Santa reads their letters.

Even if for a moment, join their world, and try not to do it with a blank face. Do it like you mean it. Like you believe it.
You don't have to pretend forever. You just need to step in long enough to let wonder rub off on both of you.

Tiny habits that keep wonder alive:

- Put a "magic box" in the kitchen. Use it for surprise notes and "official" messages from magical friends.
- After dinner, turn off the lights, look out the window, and ask, "What amazing thing did you notice today?" Then tell them yours.

- When you tuck them into bed ask one question: "What did the moon see you do today?"

And even when you are tired, playing along like this gives your children the opportunity to grow their imagination.

And you? You can feel that magical spark again.

33
Realizing That These Ordinary Days Were
the Big Moments All Along

It happens right in front of you. But you don't notice. The mornings blur into nights, the dishes into homework, and the "just a minute" into years.

You always tell yourself that you'll slow down once things calm down. Once they're older. Once work is instead of **shames** their fears easier. Once you've caught up.

But then, one evening, you find yourself scrolling through old photos ... the ones you barely remember taking.
A half-eaten birthday cake.
A crooked school project.
Your child's smile, missing teeth and all.

And it hits you:
That was it.
Those were the big moments.

It wasn't the perfect vacation or the perfect picture day.
It was the random night dance party in the kitchen.
The car ride conversations about nothing.
The messy breakfasts, the bedtime stories you almost skipped, the "one more hug" you didn't refuse.

You realize these ordinary days were never ordinary. They were everything. They were the stories you were writing without even knowing it.

⭐ Tiny habits to keep this truth close:

- At the end of each week, write down one "ordinary" moment that made you smile.
- Take more photos and when you do, step into a few of them yourself. You are a big part of this.
- Say out loud, "This is one of those small big moments." It helps your brain remember.

One day, you'll wish you could live one of these normal days all over again. You will do anything to go back and feel it more fully.

So today, while it's still right in front of you, take a breath and notice it.

Because of this, right now, in the middle of the mess, the noise, and the beautiful chaos — *is the big moment*

One day,

your house will be quiet.

No footsteps down the hallway.
No small voice calling your name from the dark.

And you won't miss the mess first.
You'll miss the moments in between—
the way they needed you
when they were half asleep
and fully sure you were their safe place.

You showed up.
Again and again.

That mattered more than you know.

Conclusion

(After You've Remembered a Few Things)

You made it to the end. Even if you just flipped through between carpools, bedtime battles, and reheated coffee.

But that's real life. That is what counts.

Not the big milestones or the smiles that are sitting in frames above the fireplace. The small, ordinary things that actually build a life.

Parenting is filled with moments that don't seem special when they are actually happening. It is dirty socks on the floor, half-eaten apples, laughter that starts right after you finish scolding someone.

In fact, parenting is grace that shows up disguised as exhaustion. And still — you're here, continually trying. Caring enough to read something like this. Wise enough to remember what really matters, even on days that don't feel pretty.

That's love, in its most reliable and true form.

And one day. When the house is quieter. When there are fever shoes lying in the garden, less finger marks on the fridge, and fewer interruptions to your thoughts...

You will have the privilege of filling that silence with every version of your child. The one who once called your name a hundred times a day, and the parent you became while answering.

So always try to remember that you don't need to chase perfect. You don't need to rush "through."

All you need to do is keep showing up, messy and human. Because that's the kind of love that leaves a mark.

And when you forget, which sometimes you will, come back here.

These 33 reminders will still be waiting for you, ready to tell you ... *you're doing better than you think.*

If any part of this book made you pause, reflect, or feel a little less alone as a parent, I would love to hear from you.

Your words matter — not just to me, but to another parent who may need to read exactly what you have to say.

If it feels right, please consider leaving a review.

Thank you for being part of this journey.
I truly appreciate your support.